Answers

compiled by
David Shibley

Tyndale House Publishers
Wheaton, Illinois

Coverdale House Publishers Ltd.
London, England

All Scripture passages quoted in
Answers are from *The Living Bible,*
© 1971 by Tyndale House Publishers,
Wheaton, Illinois.

Library of Congress Catalog
Card Number 72-97652
ISBN 8423-0080-5

Copyright © 1973 by
Tyndale House Publishers,
Wheaton, Illinois

First printing, April, 1973

Printed in the United States of America

*To my wife
Naomi
who is a visible
expression of
God's love
for me.*

CONTENTS

PART TWO
Street-Level Christianity

INTRODUCTION

Today's young people are correctly called the Searching Generation. The Christian and his message are under closer observation than ever before.

In increasing numbers young people are turning to the Bible for authoritative answers. Many authors have tried to answer the questions of youth, and God has blessed many of the books they have written. However, I felt it was time for someone to apply pertinent Scripture to the questions young people ask *without any personal comment*. The Bible, as God's written revelation to man, is in the unique position of being able to offer man a purely objective message about himself and his relationships.

It is true that the Scriptures offered here can easily be misapplied out of context. I suggest that the reader refer to the passage from which the Scriptures were taken.

Also, many of the suggestions of these verses are directed to people who know Jesus Christ as personal Lord and Savior. So some of the verses may not be applicable to the life style of a non-Christian.

Further, I have not tried to give a list of everything the Bible says about each question. Rather, I have simply shared some Scriptures that have been helpful in relation to the question being asked.

Each of these questions is a question I have been asked. If the Bible is as relevant to today's world as I believe it is, then surely it has something to say about all these questions.

It does.

David Shibley

PREFACE

That teens are asking questions is not new. It has been going on since our first family set foot on planet earth. Wasn't it in the first family that we hear a son ask, "Am I my brother's keeper?"

So long as questions are being asked, someone will have to come up with the answers.

Dave Shibley's book *Answers* is as significant as it is unique. It is significant in that Dave answers any and all the questions asked of him by this "inquiring generation."

It is unique because every question is answered directly from the Bible with a Bible quotation. Among other things, that will make all the answers correct.

David Shibley, youthful pastor and youth evangelist, has done the "now" generation a genuine service in putting into print this collection of questions and answers.

May the One who is known for his ability to ask and answer questions bless this effort with wide distribution and readership.

Carl "Kelly" Bihl, Pastor
John Brown University

PART ONE

HONEST TO GOD

1. Everyone throws a lot of different philosophies and religions at us. How can we know which one is right?

Jesus told him, "I am the Way — yes, and the Truth and the Life. No one can get to the Father except by means of me." *John 14:6*

(Jesus prayed): Make them pure and holy through teaching them your words of truth. *John 17:17*

Don't let others spoil your faith and joy with their philosophies, their wrong and shallow answers built on men's thoughts and ideas, instead of on what Christ has said. *Colossians 2:8*

2. How can I know God is alive?

The heavens are telling the glory of God; they are a marvelous display of his craftsmanship. *Psalm 19:1*

He created everything there is — nothing exists that he didn't make. *John 1:3*

Christ himself is the Creator who made everything in heaven and earth, the things we can see and the things we can't; the spirit world with its kings and kingdoms, its rulers and authorities; all were made by Christ for his own use and glory.

He was before all else began and it is his power that holds everything together.
Colossians 1:16, 17

By faith — by believing God — we know that the world and the stars — in fact, all things, were made at God's command; and that they were made from nothing!
Hebrews 11:3

You can never please God without faith, without depending on him. Anyone who wants to come to God must believe that there is a God and that he rewards those who sincerely look for him. *Hebrews 11:6*

3. How can I know God's will for my life?

Be delighted with the Lord! Then he will give you all your heart's desires. Commit everything you do to the Lord. Trust him to help you do it and he will. *Psalm 37:4, 5*

If you want favor with both God and man, and a reputation for good judgment and common sense, then trust the Lord completely; don't ever trust yourself. In everything you do, put God first, and he will direct you and crown your efforts with success. *Proverbs 3:4-6*

(An example of how to discern God's will)

Next they traveled through Phrygia and Galatia, because the Holy Spirit had told them not to go into the Turkish province of Ausia at that time. Then going along the borders of Mysia they headed north for the province of Bithynia, but again the Spirit of Jesus said no. So instead they went on through Mysia province to the city of Troas. That night Paul had a vision. In his dream he saw a man over in Macedonia, Greece, pleading with him, "Come over here and help us." Well, that settled it. We would go to Macedonia, for we could only conclude that God was sending us to preach the Good News there. *Acts 16:6-10*

And so, dear brothers, I plead with you to give your bodies to God. Let them be a living sacrifice, holy — the kind he can accept. When you think of what he has done for you, is this too much to ask? Don't copy

the behavior and customs of this
world, but be a new and
different person with a fresh
newness in all you do and think.
Then you will learn from your
own experience how his ways
will really satisfy you.
Romans 12:1, 2

For God is at work within you,
helping you want to obey
him, and then helping you do
what he wants.
Philippians 2:13

If you want to know what God
wants you to do, ask him,
and he will gladly tell
you, for he is always ready
to give a bountiful supply of
wisdom to all who ask him;
he will not resent it. But
when you ask him, be sure that
you really expect him
to tell you, for a doubtful
mind will be as unsettled as a
wave of the sea that
is driven and tossed by the
wind; and every decision you
then make will be uncertain,
as you turn first this way,
and then that. If you don't ask
with faith, don't expect the Lord
to give you any solid answer.

4. How can I know I'm going to heaven?

But to all who received him, he gave the right to become children of God. All they needed to do was to trust him to save them. *John 1:12*

For God loved the world so much that he gave his only Son so that anyone who believes in him shall not perish but have eternal life . . . And all who trust him — God's Son — to save them have eternal life; those who don't believe and obey him shall never see heaven, but the wrath of God remains upon them. *John 3:16, 36*

(Jesus said), I say emphatically that anyone who listens to my message and believes in God who sent me has eternal life, and will never be damned for his sins, but has already passed out of death into life. *John 5:24*

(Jesus said), My sheep recognize my voice, and I know them, and they follow me. I give them eternal life and they shall never perish. No one shall snatch

them away from me, for my
Father has given them to me, and
he is more powerful
than anyone else, so no one
can kidnap them from me.
John 10:27-29

But God showed his great love
for us by sending Christ
to die for us while we
were still sinners. *Romans 5:8*

So there is now no
condemnation awaiting those who
belong to Christ Jesus.
Romans 8:1

For his Holy Spirit speaks to us
deep in our hearts, and
tells us that we really are
God's children. *Romans 8:16*

And because of what Christ did,
all you others too,
who heard the Good News
about how to be saved,
and trusted Christ, were marked
as belonging to Christ
by the Holy Spirit, who long
ago had been promised to all of
us Christians.
Ephesians 1:13

Yes, dear friends, we are
already God's children, right
now, and we can't even imagine
16   what it is going to

be like later on. But we do
know this, that when
he comes we will be like him,
as a result of seeing him
as he really is. *1 John 3:2*

If we love other Christians it
proves that we have been
delivered from hell
and given eternal life. But
a person who doesn't have love
for others is headed
for eternal death. *1 John 3:14*

5. How can Christians believe that Christ is the only way to God?

Jesus told him,
"I am the Way — yes, and the
Truth and the Life. No one
can get to the Father except by
means of me." *John 14:6*

(Speaking of Christ)
There is salvation in no one
else! Under all heaven there is
no other name for men to call
upon to save them. *Acts 4:12*

God is on one side and all the
people on the other side,
and Christ Jesus, himself man, is
between them to bring
them together, by giving his life
for all mankind. This is the
message which at the proper
time God gave to the world.

17 *1 Timothy 2:5, 6*

6. How's it all going to end up?

. . . the time is coming when all the dead in their
graves shall hear the voice of God's Son, and shall rise
again — those who have done good, to eternal life;
and those who have continued in evil, to judgment.
John 5:28, 29

There are many homes up there where my Father lives, and I am going to prepare them for your coming.
When everything is ready, then I will come and get you, so that you can always be with me where I am. If this weren't so, I would tell you plainly. *John 14:2, 3*

But I am telling you this strange and wonderful secret: we shall not all die, but we shall all be given new bodies! It will all happen in a moment, in the twinkling of an eye, when the last trumpet is blown. For there will be a trumpet blast from the sky and all the Christians who have died will suddenly become alive, with new bodies that will never, never die; and then we who are still

alive shall suddenly have
new bodies too. For our
earthly bodies, the ones
we have now that can die,
must be transformed into
heavenly bodies that cannot
perish but will live forever.
When this happens, then
at last this Scripture will come
true — "Death is swallowed up
in victory."
1 Corinthians 15:51-54

7. I feel so lonely. I need a friend.

. . . God has said, "I will never,
never fail you nor forsake you."
Hebrews 13:5

Let him have all your worries
and cares, for he is always
thinking about you
and watching everything
that concerns you. *1 Peter 5:7*

8. I've really blown it and I feel so guilty. Will God really forgive me?

But some will come to me —
those the Father
has given me — and I will never,
never reject them.
John 6:37

But if we confess our sins to
him, he can be depended
on to forgive us and to
cleanse us from every wrong.

[And it is perfectly proper for God to do this for us because Christ died to wash away our sins.] *1 John 1:9*

9. I keep hearing people say that Jesus is coming back. Does the Bible give any indication as to when he will return?

. . . keep this prophecy a secret; seal it up so that it will not be understood until the end times, when travel and education shall be vastly increased! *Daniel 12:4*

Jesus told them, "Don't let anyone fool you. For many will come claiming to be the Messiah, and will lead many astray. When you hear of wars beginning, this does not signal my return; these must come, but the end is not yet. The nations and kingdoms of the earth will rise against each other and there will be famines and earthquakes in many places." *Matthew 24:4-7*

Now learn a lesson from the fig tree. When her branch is tender and the leaves begin to sprout, you know that summer is almost here. Just so, when you see all these things beginning to happen, you can know that my return is near, even at the doors. *Matthew 24:32, 33*

10. I lose out every time in my thought life. Even though I'm a Christian, I just can't keep my mind out of the gutter. Is there a way out?

The good man does not escape all troubles — he has them too. But the Lord helps him in each and every one. *Psalm 34:19*

Commit your work to the Lord, then it will succeed. *Proverbs 16:3*

Take care to live in me, and let me live in you. For a branch can't produce fruit when severed from the vine. Nor can you be fruitful apart from me. Yes, I am the Vine; you are the branches. Whoever lives in me and I in him shall produce a large crop of fruit. For apart from me you can't do a thing. *John 15:4, 5*

Since you became alive again, so to speak, when Christ arose from the dead, now set your sights on the rich treasures and joys of heaven where he sits beside God in the place of honor and power. Let heaven fill your thoughts; don't spend your time worrying about things down here. You should have as little desire for this world as a dead person does. Your real life is in heaven with Christ and God. *Colossians 3:1-3*

So give yourselves humbly to God. Resist the devil and he will flee from you. And when you draw close to God, God will draw close to you. *James 4:7, 8*

Be careful — watch out for attacks from Satan, your great enemy. He prowls around like a hungry, roaring lion, looking for some victim to tear apart. Stand firm when he attacks. Trust the Lord; and remember that other Christians all around the world are going through these sufferings too. *1 Peter 5:8, 9*

11. I have a terrible sense of guilt. How can I get rid of it?

So overflowing is his kindness toward us that he took away our sins through the blood of his Son, by whom we are saved. *Ephesians 1:7*

For he has rescued us

out of the darkness and gloom
of Satan's kingdom and
brought us into the kingdom
of his dear Son, who bought our
freedom with his blood
and forgave us all our sins.
Colossians 1:13, 14

But if we confess our sins to
him, he can be depended
on to forgive us and to
cleanse us from every
wrong. [And it is perfectly
proper for God to do this for us
because Christ died
to wash away our sins.]
1 John 1:9

And now — all glory to him
who alone is God, who saves us
through Jesus Christ our
Lord; yes, splendor and majesty,
all power and authority
are his from the beginning;
his they are and his
they evermore shall be.
And he is able to keep you
from slipping and falling
away, and to bring you,
sinless and perfect,
into his glorious presence
with mighty shouts
23   of everlasting joy. *Jude 24, 25*

12. Is God personal and approachable?

And so, dear brothers,
now we may walk right
into the very Holy of Holies
where God is, because of the
blood of Jesus.
This is the fresh, new,
life-giving way which Christ
has opened up for us by
tearing the curtain —
his human body — to let us
into the holy presence of God.
And since this great
High Priest of ours rules
over God's household, let
us go right in, to God himself,
with true hearts fully
trusting him to receive us,
because we have been
sprinkled with Christ's blood
to make us clean, and
because our bodies have
been washed with pure water.
Hebrews 10:19-22

13. Is the Bible really without error?

The whole Bible
was given to us by inspiration
from God and is useful to
teach us what is true and to
make us realize what is wrong
in our lives;
it straightens us out and
helps us do what is right.
It is God's way of

making us well prepared at
every point, fully equipped to do
good to everyone.
2 Timothy 3:16, 17

For no prophecy recorded in
Scripture was ever thought up
by the prophet himself.
It was the Holy Spirit within
these godly men who gave them
true messages from God.
2 Peter 1:20, 21

14. Is there really a hell?

Then I will turn to those on my
left and say, "Away with you,
you cursed ones, into
the eternal fire prepared for
the devil and his demons.
For I was hungry
and you wouldn't feed me;
thirsty, and you wouldn't give
me anything to drink;
a stranger, and you refused me
hospitality; naked,
and you wouldn't clothe me; sick,
and in prison, and you didn't
visit me." Then they will reply,
"Lord, when did we
ever see you hungry, or thirsty
or a stranger or naked or sick
or in prison, and did
not help you?" And I will
answer, "When you refused to

help the least of these
my brothers, you were
refusing help to me." And
they shall go away into eternal
punishment; but the righteous
into everlasting life.
Matthew 25:41-46

"There was a certain rich man,"
Jesus said, "who was splendidly
clothed and lived each day
in mirth and luxury.
One day Lazarus,
a diseased beggar, was laid
at his door. As he lay there
longing for scraps from the rich
man's table, the dogs would
come and lick his open sores.
Finally the beggar died
and was carried by the
angels to be with Abraham in
the place of the righteous
dead. The rich man also died
and was buried,
and his soul went into hell.
There, in torment, he saw
Lazarus in the far distance
with Abraham. 'Father
Abraham,' he shouted, 'have
some pity! Send Lazarus over
here if only to dip the tip of
his finger in water
and cool my tongue, for I am

in anguish in these flames.'
But Abraham said to him, 'Son,
remember that during your
lifetime you had everything
you wanted, and Lazarus
had nothing.
So now he is here being
comforted and you are in
anguish. And besides, there is
a great chasm separating us, and
anyone wanting to come
to you from here is stopped
at its edge; and no one
over there can cross to us.' "
Luke 16:19-26

I will send my angels and
they will separate out of the
Kingdom every temptation and
all who are evil,
and throw them into the furnace
and burn them. There shall
be weeping and gnashing of
teeth. *Matthew 13:41, 42*

And if anyone's name
was not found recorded in
the Book of Life, he was
thrown into the Lake of Fire.
Revelation 20:15

But cowards who turn
back from following me, and
those who are unfaithful to me,
and the corrupt and

murderers, and the immoral,
and those conversing with demons, and idol worshipers
and all liars — their doom
is in the Lake that burns
with fire and sulphur. This is
the Second Death.
Revelation 21:8

15. Show me proof that God loves me.

But God showed his great
love for us by sending Christ
to die for us while
we were still sinners.
Romans 5:8

16. What is God like?

For you must worship no other
gods, but only Jehovah,
for he is a God who claims
absolute loyalty and exclusive
devotion. *Exodus 34:14*

You must be holy because
I, the Lord your God, am
holy. *Leviticus 19:1*

But you are merciful and gentle,
Lord, slow in getting
angry, full of constant
loving-kindness and of truth.
Psalm 86:15

The Lord is watching
everywhere and keeps his eye
on both the evil and the good.
Proverbs 15:3

Holy, holy, holy is the Lord
of Hosts; the whole earth
is filled with his glory.
Isaiah 6:3

For unto us a Child is born;
unto us a Son is given;
and the government shall be
upon his shoulder. These will be
his royal titles: "Wonderful,"
"Counselor," "The Mighty
God," "The Everlasting Father,"
"The Prince of Peace."
His ever-expanding, peaceful
government will never end.
He will rule with perfect
fairness and justice from the
throne of his father David.
He will bring true justice and
peace to all the nations
of the world. This is going to
happen because the Lord of
heaven's armies has
dedicated himself to do it!
Isaiah 9:6, 7

(Jesus said), "Anyone who has
seen me has seen the Father!"
John 14:9

He made the world and
everything in it, and since he
is Lord of heaven and earth,
he doesn't live in
29   man-made temples; and human

hands can't minister to his
needs — for he has no needs!
He himself gives life and breath
to everything, and satisfies every
need there is. He created
all the people of the
world from one man, Adam, and
scattered the nations
across the face of the earth.
He decided beforehand which
should rise and fall, and when.
He determined their boundaries.
His purpose in all of this
is that they should
seek after God, and perhaps
feel their way toward him
and find him — though
he is not far from any one
of us. For in him we live and
move and are!
Acts 17:24-28a

Don't you realize how patient he
is being with you? Or don't
you care? Can't you see
that he has been waiting all
this time without punishing you,
to give you time to turn
from your sin? His kindness
is meant to lead you to
repentance. *Romans 2:4*

For God sent Christ Jesus to
take the punishment for our
sins and to end

all God's anger against us.
He used Christ's blood and
our faith as the means of saving
us from his wrath. In this
way he was being entirely fair,
even though he did not
punish those who sinned in
former times. For he
was looking forward to the time
when Christ would come
and take away those sins.
And now in these
days also he can receive sinners
in this same way,
because Jesus took away
their sins. But isn't this unfair
for God to let criminals go free,
and say that they are innocent?
No, for he does it
on the basis of their trust
in Jesus who took away their sins.
Romans 3:25, 26

. . . for we know
how dearly God loves us, and we
feel this warm love everywhere
within us because God
has given us the Holy Spirit
to fill our hearts with his love.
Romans 5:5

Oh, what a wonderful God we
have! How great are his
wisdom and knowledge

and riches! How impossible
it is for us to understand
his decisions and his
methods! *Romans 11:33*

Long ago, even before he made
the world, God chose us to
be his very own,
through what Christ would do
for us; he decided then to make
us holy in his eyes,
without a single fault —
we who stand before him
covered with his love.
Ephesians 1:4

He was before all else
began and it is his power
that holds everything together.
Colossians 1:17

Even when we are too weak to
have any faith left, he remains
faithful to us and will help
us, for he cannot disown us
who are part of himself,
and he will always
carry out his promises to us.
2 Timothy 2:13

This High Priest of ours
understands our weaknesses,
since he had the same
temptations we do, though
32 he never once gave way to

them and sinned.
Hebrews 4:15

This is the message God has
given us to pass on to you: that
God is Light and in him is
no darkness at all. *1 John 1:5*

We know how much God
loves us because we
have felt his love and because
we believe him when he tells
us that he loves us dearly. God
is love, and anyone who
lives in love is living with God
and God is living in him.
1 John 4:16

After this I heard the shouting
of a vast crowd in heaven,
"Hallelujah! Praise the
Lord! Salvation is from our
God. Honor and authority
belong to him alone;
for his judgments are just
and true." *Revelation 19:1, 2*

17. What's the real difference between a Christian and a non-Christian?

But to all who received him he gave the right
to become children of God.
All they needed to do was to trust him to save them.
John 1:12

When someone becomes a Christian he becomes a
brand new person inside.
He is not the same anymore.
A new life has begun!
2 Corinthians 5:17

18. What is the ultimate goal of the Christian life?

For from the very beginning God decided that those who
came to him — and all along
he knew who would —
should become like his
Son, so that his Son would
be the First, with many brothers.
Romans 8:29

(Jesus Christ) died under God's judgment against our sins,
so that he could
rescue us from constant falling into sin and make us
his very own people, with
cleansed hearts and real
enthusiasm for doing kind
things for others. *Titus 2:14*

19. What makes Christianity so different from any other religion?

Yes, all have sinned;
all fall short of God's glorious
ideal; yet now God declares us
"not guilty" of offending him if
we trust in Jesus Christ,
who in his kindness
freely takes away our sins.
Romans 3:23, 24

I passed on to you right from
the first what had been told
to me, that Christ died
for our sins just as the
Scriptures said he would, and
that he was buried, and that three
days afterwards he arose from
the grave just as the
prophets foretold.
1 Corinthians 15:3, 4

Because of his kindness you
have been saved through
trusting Christ. And even trusting is not of yourselves;
it too is a gift from God.
Salvation is not a
reward for the good we have
done, so none of us
can take any credit for it.
Ephesians 2:8, 9

20. Why would a loving God send anyone to hell?

God did not send his Son into the world to condemn it, but to save it. There is no eternal doom awaiting those who trust him to save them. But those who don't trust him have already been tried and condemned for not believing in the only Son of God. *John 3:17, 18*

PART TWO

STREET-LEVEL
CHRISTIANITY

1. Christians really confuse me — especially on issues of personal conviction. How can I know if it's right to participate in certain activities?

You have no right to criticize your brother or look down on him. Remember, each of us will stand personally before the Judgment Seat of God. For it is written, "As I live," says the Lord, "Every knee shall bow to me and every tongue confess to God." Yes, each of us will give an account of himself to God. So don't criticize each other any more. Try instead to live in such a way that you will never make your brother stumble by letting him see you doing something he thinks is wrong.

As for myself, I am perfectly sure on the authority of the Lord Jesus that there is nothing really wrong with eating meat that has been offered to idols. But if someone believes it is wrong, then he shouldn't do it because for him it is wrong. And if your brother is bothered by what you eat, you are not acting in love if you go ahead and eat it. Don't let your eating

ruin someone for whom
Christ died. Don't do anything
that will cause criticism
against yourself even
though you know that
what you do is right.
Romans 14:10-16

The right thing to do is to quit
eating meat or drinking wine
or doing anything else
that offends your brother
or makes him sin.
You may know that
there is nothing wrong
with what you do, even
from God's point of view,
but keep it to yourself;
don't flaunt your faith
in front of others who
might be hurt by it. In this
situation, happy is the man who
does not sin by doing what he
knows is right. But
anyone who believes that
something he wants
to do is wrong shouldn't do it.
He sins if he does,
for he thinks it is wrong,
and so for him it is wrong.
Anything that is done
apart from what he
feels is right is sin.

39   *Romans 14:21-23*

So now, what about it?
Should we eat meat that
has been sacrificed to idols?
Well, we all know that an idol
is not really a god,
and that there is only one
God, and no other.
According to some people, there
are a great many gods, both in
heaven and on earth.
But we know that there
is only one God, the Father,
who created all things and made
us to be his own; and one Lord
Jesus Christ, who made everything and gives us life.

However, some Christians
don't realize this.
All their lives they have been
used to thinking of idols as
alive, and have believed
that food offered to the idols is
really being offered to
actual gods. So when they eat
such food it bothers them and
hurts their tender consciences.
Just remember that God doesn't
care whether we eat it or
not. We are no worse off
if we don't eat it, and no better
off if we do. But be careful
not to use your freedom

to eat it, lest you cause some

Christian brother to sin whose
conscience is weaker than yours.
   You see, this is what may
happen: Someone who thinks it
is wrong to eat this food will see
you eating at a
temple restaurant, for you
know there is no harm in it.
Then he will become bold
enough to do it too, although all
the time he still feels it is wrong.
So because you
"know it is all right to do it,"
you will be responsible
for causing great spiritual
damage to a brother with a
tender conscience for whom
Christ died. And it is sin
against Christ to sin against
your brother by encouraging him
to do something
he thinks is wrong. So if
eating meat offered to idols is
going to make my brother
sin, I'll not eat any of it as
long as I live,
because I don't want to do this
to him. *1 Corinthians 8:4-13*

And whatever you do or say,
let it be as a representative
of the Lord Jesus,
and come with him into the
presence of God the Father

to give him your thanks.
Colossians 3:17

2. What advice do you have on bridging the "Generation Gap"?

And so I am giving a new
commandment to you now —
love each other
just as much as I love you.
Your strong love for
each other will prove to the
world that you are my disciples.
John 1:34, 35

3. Does the Bible tell how I can find real freedom?

Jesus said to them, "You are
truly my disciples if you live
as I tell you to,
and you will know the truth,
and the truth will set you free."
   "But we are descendants
of Abraham," they said,
"and have never been
slaves to any man on earth!
What do you mean, 'set free'?"
   Jesus replied,
"You are slaves of sin,
every one of you.
And slaves don't have rights, but
the Son has every right there
is! So if the Son sets you free,
you will indeed be free."

John 8:31-36

4. Home for me is hell. My parents and I just don't get along. But I'm trying to have a right attitude. What can I do?

. . . be kind to each other, tenderhearted, forgiving one another, just as God has forgiven you because you belong to Christ. *Ephesians 4:32*

Children, obey your parents; this is the right thing to do because God has placed them in authority over you. Honor your father and mother. This is the first of God's Ten Commandments that ends with a promise. And this is the promise: that if you honor your father and mother, yours will be a long life, full of blessing. *Ephesians 6:1-3*

5. How can I be happy?

God blesses those who obey him; happy the man who puts his trust in the Lord. *Proverbs 16:20*

Happy are those whose God is Jehovah. *Psalm 144:15*

6. How can I make my life really count?

Constantly remind the people about these laws, and you yourself must think about them every day and every night so that you will be sure

43

to obey all of them. For
only then will you succeed.
Joshua 1:8

Be delighted with the Lord!
Then he will give
you all your heart's desires.
Commit everything you do to the
Lord. Trust him to help you
do it and he will.
Psalm 37:4, 5

If you want favor with both
God and man,
and a reputation for good
judgment and common sense,
then trust the Lord
completely; don't ever trust
yourself. In everything you do,
put God first,
and he will direct you and
crown your efforts with success.
Don't be conceited, sure
of your own wisdom. Instead,
trust and reverence the Lord,
and turn your back on evil;
when you do that, then you
will be given renewed health and
vitality. *Proverbs 3:4-8*

Above all else, guard
your affections. For they
influence everything else in
your life. *Proverbs 4:23*

Ill-gotten gain brings
no lasting happiness;
right living does.
Proverbs 10:2

The path of the godly
leads to life. So why fear death?
Proverbs 12:28

Reverence for the Lord is a
fountain of life; its waters keep
a man from death.
Proverbs 14:27

Humility and reverence for
the Lord will make you both
wise and honored.
Proverbs 15:33

Commit your work
to the Lord, then it will
succeed. *Proverbs 16:3*

The man who tries to be
good, loving and kind finds life,
righteousness and honor.
Proverbs 21:21

True humility and respect for
the Lord lead a man to
riches, honor and long life.
Proverbs 22:4

7. How does the Bible stand on capital punishment?

. . . any man who murders shall be killed; for to kill a man is to kill one made like God.
Genesis 9:6

8. I'm hooked on drugs. Can you please help me?

The Lord is a strong fortress. The godly run to him and are safe.
Proverbs 18:10

Yes, I am the Vine; you are the branches. Whoever lives in me and I in him shall produce a large crop of fruit. For apart from me you can't do a thing.
John 15:5

So look upon your old sin nature as dead and unresponsive to sin, and instead be alive to God, alert to him, through Jesus Christ our Lord.
Do not let sin control your puny body any longer; do not give in to its sinful desires. Do not let any part of your bodies become tools of wickedness, to be used for sinning; but give

yourselves completely to
God — every part of you —
for you are back from death
and you want to be tools
in the hands of God, to be
used for his good purposes.
Sin need never again be your
master, for now you
are no longer tied to the law
where sin enslaves you,
but you are free
under God's favor and mercy.
Romans 6:11-14

The God of peace will soon
crush Satan under your feet.
Romans 16:20a

In every battle you will need
faith as your shield
to stop the fiery arrows aimed
at you by Satan.
Ephesians 6:16

Always be full of joy in the
Lord; I say it again, rejoice!
Philippians 4:4

You were dead in sins,
and your sinful desires
were not yet cut away.
Then he gave you a share in
the very life of Christ,
for he forgave all your sins, and
blotted out the charges proved

against you, the list of
his commandments which you
had not obeyed. He took
this list of sins and destroyed it
by nailing it to Christ's cross.
In this way God took away
Satan's power to accuse you of
sin, and God openly displayed
to the whole world
Christ's triumph at the cross
where your sins were all
taken away.
Colossians 2:13-15

So give yourselves humbly to
God. Resist the devil and
he will flee from you. *James 4:7*

But if we confess our sins to
him, he can be depended on
to forgive us
and to cleanse us from
every wrong. [And it is
perfectly proper for
God to do this for us
because Christ died to wash
away our sins.] *1 John 1:9*

And now — all glory to him
who alone is God,
who saves us through Jesus
Christ our Lord; yes, splendor
and majesty, all power
and authority are his from
the beginning; his they are and

his they evermore shall
be. And he is able to keep
you from slipping and
falling away, and to bring
you, sinless and perfect,
into his glorious
presence with mighty shouts of
everlasting joy. *Jude 24, 25*

They defeated him by the
blood of the Lamb,
and by their testimony; for they
did not love their lives but
laid them down for him.
Revelation 12:11

9. I'm scared to death of the future. With the threat of nuclear war and total annihilation, where can I run to?

For the Lord is with you;
he protects you.
Proverbs 3:26

We live within the
shadow of the Almighty,
sheltered by the God who is
above all gods.
This I declare, that he alone
is my refuge, my place of
safety; he is my God,
and I am trusting him. For he
rescues you from every trap
and protects you from
the fatal plague. He will shield
you with his wings!
They will shelter you.
His faithful promises are your

armor. Now you don't need to
be afraid of the dark
any more, nor fear the
dangers of the day; nor dread
the plagues of darkness,
nor disasters in the morning.
  Though a thousand fall at my
side, though ten thousand
are dying around me,
the evil will not touch me.
I will see how the wicked
are punished but I
will not share it. For Jehovah
is my refuge! I choose
the God above all gods
to shelter me. How then
can evil overtake me or any
plague come near? For he
orders his angels to protect you
wherever you go.
They will steady you with their
hands to keep you from
stumbling against the rocks on
the trail. You can safely
meet a lion or step on poisonous
snakes; yes, even trample them
beneath your feet!
  For the Lord says, "Because
he loves me, I will rescue him;
I will make him great
because he trusts in my name.
When he calls on me
50 I will answer; I will be with him

in trouble, and rescue him
and honor him.
I will satisfy him with a full life
and give him my
salvation." *Psalm 91*

10. I'm under such pressure from my parents to make good grades, I find myself stealing answers on tests. But under the circumstances, isn't it all right?

. . . you know the commandments: don't kill, don't commit adultery, don't steal, don't lie, don't cheat, respect your father and mother." *Mark 10:19*

You tell others not to steal — do *you* steal? *Romans 2:21*

If you love your neighbor as much as you love yourself you will not want to harm or cheat him, or kill him or steal from him. *Romans 13:9*

If anyone is stealing he must stop it and begin using those hands of his for honest work so he can give to others in need. *Ephesians 4:28*

51

11. I just found out some pretty terrible things about this "great" Christian guy. I placed so much faith in him and he's failed me so miserably. After this, how can I believe Christianity is real?

Keep your eyes on Jesus, our leader and instructor. *Hebrews 12:2*

12. I want a challenge big enough to throw my whole life into: my time, my money, my energy, my abilities, everything. Would the Christian life provide that challenge?

Jesus called out,
"Come along with me and I
will show you how to fish for
the souls of men!" *Matthew 4:19*

He told his disciples, "I have
been given all authority
in heaven and earth.
Therefore go and make
disciples in all the nations,
baptizing them into the
name of the Father and of
the Son and of the
Holy Spirit, and then teach
these new disciples to
obey all the commands
I have given you; and
be sure of this — that I am
with you always,
even to the end of the world."
Matthew 28:18-20

The Spirit of the Lord is upon
me; he has appointed me
to preach Good News
to the poor; he has sent me
to announce that captives
shall be released and
the blind shall see,
that the downtrodden shall
be freed from their oppressors,
and that God is ready to give
blessings to all who
come to him. *Luke 4:18, 19*

53

. . . to open their eyes
to their true condition
so that they may repent and live
in the light of God instead
of Satan's darkness, so that
they may receive forgiveness for
their sins and God's inheritance
along with all people everywhere
whose sins are cleansed away,
who are set apart
by faith in me. *Acts 26:18*

13. If the Christian life is so great, why do I, as a Christian, have so many problems?

These troubles and sufferings
of ours are, after all,
quite small and won't last
very long. Yet this short time
of distress will result
in God's richest blessing
upon us forever and ever!
So we do not look at what
we can see right now,
the troubles all around us,
but we look forward
to the joys in heaven which
we have not yet seen.
The troubles will soon
be over, but the joys to
come will last forever.
2 Corinthians 4:17, 18

". . . I am with you;
that is all you need.

My power shows up best in weak

people." Now I am glad to
boast about how weak I am;
I am glad to be a living
demonstration of Christ's power,
instead of showing off
my own power and abilities.
Since I know it is all
for Christ's good, I am
quite happy about "the
thorn," and about insults and
hardships, persecutions and
difficulties; for when
I am weak, then I am strong —
the less I have, the more
I depend on him.
2 Corinthians 12:9, 10

These trials are only to test
your faith, to see whether or not
it is strong and pure. It is being tested as fire tests gold and
purifies it — and your faith is far
more precious to God than
mere gold; so if your faith
remains strong after being
tried in the test tube of fiery
trials, it will bring you much
praise and glory and honor on
the day of his return.
1 Peter 1:7

14. I'm not popular. I feel rejected and insecure. Honestly, does anyone really love me?

Come to me and I will give you rest — all of you who work so hard beneath a heavy yoke. Wear my yoke — for it fits perfectly — and let me teach you; for I am gentle and humble, and you shall find rest for your souls; for I give you only light burdens. *Matthew 11:28-30*

But God showed his great love for us by sending Christ to die for us while we were still sinners. *Romans 5:8*

15. Sometimes I wonder just why I am here, anyway.

For from the very beginning God decided that those who came to him — and all along he knew who would — should become like his Son, so that his Son would be the First, with many brothers. *Romans 8:29*

And this is what God says we must do: believe on the name of his Son Jesus Christ, and love one another. *1 John 3:23*

16. What are the real values in life?

Determination to be wise is the first step toward becoming wise! And with your wisdom, develop common sense and good judgment.
Proverbs 4:7

Above all else, guard your affections. For they influence everything else in your life.
Proverbs 4:23

I love all who love me. Those who search for me shall surely find me. Unending riches, honor, justice and righteousness are mine to distribute. My gifts are better than the purest gold or sterling silver! My paths are those of justice and right. Those who love and follow me are indeed wealthy. I fill their treasuries.
Proverbs 8:17-21

Ill-gotten gain brings no lasting happiness; right living does. *Proverbs 10:2*

Godly men are growing a tree that bears life-giving fruit, and all who win souls are wise.
Proverbs 11:30

The path of the godly leads to life. So why fear death?
Proverbs 12:28

Here is my final conclusion:
fear God and obey his
commandments; for this is the
entire duty of man.
Ecclesiastes 12:13

He has told you what he wants,
and this is all it is: to be
fair and just and merciful, and
to walk humbly with your God.
Micah 6:8

And this is the way to have
eternal life — by knowing you,
the only true God, and Jesus
Christ, the one you sent to earth!
John 17:3

17. What can the Christian do to help improve race relations?

Be kind to each other,
tenderhearted, forgiving
one another, just as God has
forgiven you because
you belong to Christ.
Ephesians 4:32

18. What should the Christian's position be in the ecological issue?

And God blessed them and told
them, "Multiply and fill the earth
and subdue it; you are masters
of the fish and birds and all
the animals. And look! I have
given you the seed-bearing
plants throughout the earth, and
all the fruit trees for your

food. And I've given all the
grass and plants to the animals
and birds for their food."
Genesis 1:38-40

You have put him in
charge of everything you made;
everything is put under his
authority: all sheep and oxen,
and wild animals too, the
birds and fish, and all the life in
the sea. *Psalm 8:6-8*

And if God cares so wonderfully
for flowers that are here
today and gone tomorrow, won't
he more surely care for you,
O men of little faith?
Matthew 6:30

19. What should the Christian's response be to the poverty problem?

God blesses those who are kind
to the poor. *Psalm 41:1a*

To despise the poor is to
sin. Blessed are those who pity
them. *Proverbs 14:21*

To help the poor is to honor
God. *Proverbs 14:31b*

But if someone who is supposed
to be a Christian has money
enough to live well, and sees a
brother in need, and won't
help him — how can God's love
be within him? Little children,

let us stop just saying
we love people; let us really
love them, and show it by our
actions. *1 John 3:17, 18*

**20. I became a
Christian last
year, and I
really am glad
I have Christ
in my life —
but I feel as if I
am at a real
standstill; what
can I do to
become a
better
Christian,
more mature
and stable?**

(I pray) that out of his
glorious, unlimited resources he
will give you the mighty inner
strengthening of his Holy
Spirit. And I pray that Christ
will be more and more at
home in your hearts, living
within you as you trust in him.
May your roots go down deep
into the soil of God's marvelous
love. . . . *Ephesians 3:16, 17*

When the Holy Spirit controls
our lives he will produce this
kind of fruit in us: love, joy,
peace, patience, kindness,
goodness, faithfulness,
gentleness and self-control.
Galatians 5:22, 23

I don't mean to say I am perfect.
I haven't learned all I
should even yet, but I keep
working toward that day when I
will finally be all that Christ
saved me for and wants me to
be. No, dear brothers, I am
still not all I should be but I am
bringing all my energies to bear

on this one thing: Forgetting
the past and looking forward to
what lies ahead, I strain to reach
the end of the race and
receive the prize for which
God is calling us up to heaven
because of what Christ Jesus did
for us. *Philippians 3:12-14*

And now just as you trusted
Christ to save you, trust him,
too, for each day's problems; live
in vital union with him. Let
your roots grow down into him
and draw up nourishment from
him. See that you go on growing
in the Lord, and become strong
and vigorous in the truth you
were taught. Let your lives
overflow with joy and thanks-
giving for all he has done.
Colossians 2:6, 7

Knowing what lies ahead for
you, you won't become bored
with being a Christian, nor
become spiritually dull and
indifferent, but you will be
anxious to follow the example of
those who receive all that
God has promised them because
of their strong faith and
patience. *Hebrews 6:12*

Do you want more and more of

God's kindness and peace?
Then learn to know him better
and better. For as you know
him better, he will give you,
through his great power,
everything you need for living a
truly good life: he even shares
his own glory and his own
goodness with us! And by that
same mighty power he has given
us all the other rich and
wonderful blessings he promised;
for instance, the promise to
save us from the lust and
rottenness all around us, and to
give us his own character.

But to obtain these gifts,
you need more than faith; you
must also work hard to be good,
and even that is not enough.
For then you must
learn to know God better and
discover what he wants you to do.
Next, learn to put aside your
own desires so that you will
become patient and godly,
gladly letting God have his way
with you. This will make
possible the next step, which is
for you to enjoy other people
and to like them, and
finally you will grow to love them
deeply. The more you go

on in this way, the more you
will grow strong spiritually and
become fruitful and useful
to our Lord Jesus Christ.
2 Peter 1:2-8

21. I don't quite understand what the Bible is supposed to do for me. Why is it so important for me to read it?

How can a young man stay
pure? By reading your Word and
following its rules . . . Blessed
Lord, teach me your rules. I have
recited your laws, and
rejoiced in them more than in
riches. I will meditate upon
them and give them my full
respect. I will delight in
them and not forget them . . .
I am completely discouraged —
I lie in the dust. Revive me
by your Word . . . Your words are
a flashlight to light the
path ahead of me, and keep
me from stumbling.
Psalm 119:9, 12-16, 25, 105

The whole Bible was given to us
by inspiration from God
and is useful to teach us what
is true and to make us realize
what is wrong in our lives; it
straightens us out and
helps us do what is right.
It is God's way of making
us well prepared at every point,

fully equipped to do
good to everyone.
2 Timothy 3:16, 17

22. What should I talk to God about when I pray?

Pray all the time. Ask God for
anything in line with the
Holy Spirit's wishes. Plead with
him, reminding him of your
needs, and keep praying earnestly
for all Christians everywhere.
Ephesians 6:18

Don't worry about anything;
instead, pray about
everything; tell God your
needs and don't forget to thank
him for his answers.
Philippians 4:6

Don't be weary in prayer; keep
at it; watch for God's answers
and remember to be thankful
when they come.
Colossians 4:2

Here are my directions:
Pray much for others; plead for
God's mercy upon them; give
thanks for all he is going to
do for them. Pray in this way
for kings and all others who are
in authority over us, or are in
places of high responsibility, so
that we can live in peace and
quietness, spending our time

in godly living and thinking much about the Lord.
1 Timothy 2:1, 2

If you want to know what God wants you to do, ask him, and he will gladly tell you, for he is always ready to give a bountiful supply of wisdom to all who ask him; he will not resent it. But when you ask him, be sure that you really expect him to tell you, for a doubtful mind will be as unsettled as a wave of the sea that is driven and tossed by the wind; and every decision you then make will be uncertain, as you turn first this way, and then that. If you don't ask with faith, don't expect the Lord to give you any solid answer.
James 1:5-8

23. Can't I be a Christian without going to church? I get nothing out of church; it seems dead to me.

Why is it that he gives us these special abilities to do certain things best? It is that God's people will be equipped to do better work for him, building up the church, the body of Christ, to a position of strength and maturity; until finally we all believe alike about our salvation and about

our Savior, God's Son, and all
become full-grown in the Lord —
yes, to the point of being
filled full with Christ . . . We will
lovingly follow the truth
at all times —
speaking truly, dealing truly,
living truly — and so become
more and more in every way
like Christ who is the Head
of his body, the church. Under
his direction the whole body
is fitted together perfectly,
and each part in its own
special way helps the other
parts, so that the whole body is
healthy and growing and full of
love. *Ephesians 4:12, 13, 15, 16*

Remember what Christ taught
and let his words enrich
your lives and make you wise;
teach them to each other and
sing songs, singing to the Lord
with thankful hearts.
Colossians 3:16

In response to all he has done
for us, let us outdo each
other in being helpful and kind
to each other and in doing
good. Let us not neglect our
church meetings, as some
people do, but encourage and

warn each other, especially now
that the day of his coming back
again is drawing near.
Hebrews 10:24, 25

Just as there are many parts
to our bodies, so it is with
Christ's body. We are all parts
of it, and it takes every one of
us to make it complete,
for we each have different work
to do. So we belong to each
other, and each needs all the
others. *Romans 12:4, 5*

Now here is what I am
trying to say: All of you
together are the one body of
Christ and each one of you
is a separate and necessary
part of it. Here is a list of some
of the parts he has placed in
his church, which is his body:
Apostles, prophets — those
who preach God's Word,
teachers, those who do miracles,
those who have the gift
of healing, those who can help
others, those who can get
others to work together, those
who speak in languages they
have never learned.
1 Corinthians 12:27, 28

PART THREE

ON FINDING
THE BEAUTIFUL
BETWEEN A MAN
AND A WOMAN

1. Although I'm a Christian I'm in love with a non-Christian. Should we get married?

Don't be teamed with those who do not love the Lord, for what do the people of God have in common with the people of sin? How can light live with darkness? . . . How can a Christian be a partner with one who doesn't believe? *2 Corinthians 6:14*

2. How can I be sure I'll have a happy home and married life?

Honor your marriage and its vows, and be pure; for God will surely punish all those who are immoral or commit adultery. *Hebrews 13:4*

Let there be no sex sin, impurity or greed among you. Let no one be able to accuse you of any such things. *Ephesians 5:3*

Advice on the correction of children

If you refuse to discipline your son, it proves you don't love him; for if you love him you will be prompt to punish him. *Proverbs 13:24*

A youngster's heart is filled with rebellion, but punishment will drive it out of him. *Proverbs 22:15*

Don't keep on scolding and nagging your children, making them angry and resentful. Rather, bring them up with the loving discipline the Lord himself approves, with suggestions and godly advice. *Ephesians 6:4*

Advice to husbands

Let your manhood be a blessing; rejoice in the wife of your youth. Let her charms and tender embrace satisfy you. Let her love alone fill you with delight. Why delight yourself with prostitutes, embracing what isn't yours? For God is closely watching you, and he weighs carefully everything you do. *Proverbs 5:18-21*

Live happily with the woman you love through the fleeting days of life, for the wife God gives you is your best reward down here for all your earthly toil. *Ecclesiastes 9:9*

And you husbands, show the same kind of love to your wives as Christ showed to the church when he died for her, to make her holy and clean,

washed by baptism and
God's Word; so that he could
give her to himself as a glorious
church without a single spot or
wrinkle or any other blemish,
being holy and without a
single fault. That is how
husbands should treat their
wives, loving them as parts of
themselves. For since a man and
his wife are now one, a man
is really doing himself a favor
and loving himself when he
loves his wife! No one
hates his own body but
lovingly cares for it, just as
Christ cares for his body the
church, of which we are parts.

(That the husband and wife
are one body is proved by the
Scripture which says, "A man
must leave his father and
mother when he marries, so
that he can be perfectly joined to
his wife, and the two shall be
one.") *Ephesians 5:25-31*

And you husbands
must be loving and kind to
your wives and not bitter against
them, nor harsh. *Colossians 3:19*

You husbands must be careful
71 of your wives, being thoughtful

of their needs and honoring them as the weaker sex. Remember that you and your wife are partners in receiving God's blessings, and if you don't treat her as you should, your prayers will not get ready answers. *1 Peter 3:7*

Advice to wives

If you can find a truly good wife, she is worth more than precious gems. Her husband can trust her, and she will richly satisfy his needs. She will not hinder him, but help him all her life. She finds wool and flax and busily spins it. She buys imported foods, brought by ship from distant ports. She gets up before dawn to prepare breakfast for her household, and plans the day's work for her servant girls. She goes out to inspect a field, and buys it; with her own hands she plants a vineyard. She is energetic, a hard worker, and watches for bargains. She works far into the night!

She sews for the poor, and generously gives to the needy. She has no fear of winter for her household, for she has

72

made warm clothes for all of
them. She also upholsters with
finest tapestry; her own clothing
is beautifully made — a purple
gown of pure linen.
Her husband is well known, for
he sits in the council chamber
with the other civic leaders. She
makes belted linen garments
to sell to the merchants.

She is a woman of strength
and dignity, and has no
fear of old age. When she
speaks, her words are wise, and
kindness is the rule for
everything she says. She
watches carefully all that goes
on throughout her household,
and is never lazy. Her children
stand and bless her;
so does her husband. He praises
her with these words: "There
are many fine women in the
world, but you are the best of
them all!"

Charm can be deceptive and
beauty doesn't last, but a
woman who fears and reverences
God shall be greatly praised.
Praise her for the many fine
things she does. These good
deeds of hers shall bring her
honor and recognition from even

the leaders of the nation.
Proverbs 31:10-31

You wives must submit to your
husbands' leadership in the
same way you submit to the Lord.
For a husband is in charge
of his wife in the same way Christ
is in charge of his body
the church. (He gave his very
life to take care of it and be
its Savior!) So you wives must
willingly obey your husbands in
everything, just as the church
obeys Christ. *Ephesians 5:22-24*

Wives, fit in with your
husbands' plans; for then if
they refuse to listen when you
talk to them about the Lord, they
will be won by your respectful,
pure behavior. Your godly lives
will speak to them better
than any words.

Don't be concerned about
the outward beauty that depends
on jewelry, or beautiful clothes,
or hair arrangement. Be
beautiful inside, in your hearts,
with the lasting charm of a gentle
and quiet spirit which is so
precious to God. *1 Peter 3:1-4*

Causes of family trouble

Dishonest money brings grief to all the family, but hating bribes brings happiness.
Proverbs 15:27

Laziness lets the roof leak, and soon the rafters begin to rot.
Ecclesiastes 10:18

You were united to your wife by the Lord. In God's wise plan, when you married, the two of you became one person in his sight. And what does he want? Godly children from your union. Therefore guard your passions! Keep faith with the wife of your youth.
Malachi 2:15

Advice to children

The character of even a child can be known by the way he acts — whether what he does is pure and right.
Proverbs 20:11

Listen to your father's advice and don't despise an old mother's experience.
Proverbs 23:22

Don't let the excitement of being young cause you
to forget about your Creator.

Honor him in your youth before
the evil years come —
when you'll no longer enjoy
living. *Ecclesiastes 12:1*

Children, obey your parents;
this is the right thing
to do because God
has placed them in authority
over you. Honor your father
and mother. This is the first
of God's Ten Commandments
that ends with a promise.
And this is the promise:
that if you honor
your father and mother,
yours will be a long life,
full of blessing.
Ephesians 6:1-3

*3. I'm
pregnant.
I've got
syphilis.
How can a
holy God
love me
anymore?*

He forgives all my sins.
He heals me. He ransoms me
from hell. He surrounds me
with lovingkindness and
tender mercies.
He fills my life with good
things! My youth is renewed
like the eagle's! . . . He is
merciful and tender toward
those who don't deserve it;
he is slow to get angry and full
of kindness and love . . .
He has not punished us

as we deserve for all our sins,
for his mercy toward those
who fear and honor him
is as great as the height of
the heavens above the earth.
He has removed our sins
as far away from us as the east
is from the west.
Psalm 103:3-5, 8, 10-12

It is a broken spirit you want —
remorse and penitence.
A broken and a contrite heart,
O God, you will not ignore.
Psalm 51:17

Come, let's talk this over!
says the Lord; no matter
how deep the stain
of your sins, I can take it
out and make you as clean as
freshly fallen snow.
Even if you are stained as red as
crimson, I can make you white
as wool! *Isaiah 1:18*

But for you who fear my Name,
the Sun of Righteousness
will rise with healing
in his wings. And you
will go free, leaping with
joy like calves let out to
pasture. *Malachi 4:2*

Come to me and I will give you
rest — all of you who work so

hard beneath a heavy yoke.
Wear my yoke — for it fits
perfectly, and let me teach you;
for I am gentle and humble,
and you shall find rest for
your souls; for I give you only
light burdens. *Matthew 11:28-30*

**4. I've just
been shut
down
completely by
the person I
love and I feel
like God could
care less.**

Great is his faithfulness;
his lovingkindness begins afresh
each day. *Lamentations 3:23*

. . . God has said, "I will
never, never fail you nor
forsake you." *Hebrews 13:5*

O Jehovah, Commander of the
heavenly armies, where is there
any other Mighty One like you?
Faithfulness is your
very character. *Psalm 89:8*

**5. The Bible
never says
anything
against
premarital
sex, does it?**

Sexual sin is never right:
our bodies were not made for
that, but for the Lord . . .
That is why I say to run from
sex sin. No other sin affects the
body as this one does.
When you sin this sin it is
against your own body.
1 Corinthians 6:13b, 18

I advise you to obey only the
Holy Spirit's instructions. He

will tell you where to go and
what to do, and then you
won't always be doing the wrong
things your evil nature wants
you to. *Galatians 5:16*

Let there be no sex sin, impurity
or greed among you. Let no one
be able to accuse you
of any such things.
Ephesians 5:3

Away then with sinful, earthly
things; deaden the evil desires
lurking within you; have
nothing to do with sexual sin,
impurity, lust and shameful
desires; don't worship the good
things of life, for that is
idolatry. God's terrible anger is
upon those who do such
things. *Colossians 3:5, 6*

For God wants you to be holy
and pure, and to keep clear
of all sexual sin so that
each of you will marry in holiness
and honor — not in lustful
passion as the heathen do, in
their ignorance of God
and his ways.
1 Thessalonians 4:3-5

6. What is real love like?

Love is very patient and kind, never jealous or envious, never boastful or proud, never haughty or selfish or rude. Love does not demand its own way. It is not irritable or touchy. It does not hold grudges and will hardly even notice when others do it wrong. It is never glad about injustice, but rejoices whenever truth wins out. If you love someone you will be loyal to him no matter what the cost. You will always believe in him, always expect the best of him, and always stand your ground in defending him.

1 Corinthians 13:4-7